THE BURNING WORD

THE
BURNING WORD

Poems & Songs

JEHANNE MEHTA

The Diamond Press
London 1991

First published in Great Britain
by the Diamond Press
5 Berners Mansions
34-36 Berners Street
London W1

© Jehanne Mehta 1988, 1989, 1990, 1991
All rights reserved

Cover lettering Jojo Mehta
Cover drawing Jehanne Mehta
Decorations by Arthur Mehta

Photoset in Mergenthaler Galliard
at Five Seasons Press
Printed on 100% recycled Five Seasons book paper
by Whitstable Litho, Kent

ISBN 0 948684 05 4

To
the Theogamy, being the god-marriage
between the love which converges from without
and the love which emerges from within:
'The point where we are together
is the point where everything
begins'

For Z

In the new mysteries the whole Earth becomes a temple. The hidden tragedy and triumph of the pupil begin to become external fact. A man's own friends begin to become for him—though he may know little of it—the terrible and wonderful actors in the ceremony of his initiation.

RUDOLF STEINER

Resolute Imagination can accomplish all things.

PARACELSUS

I am giving you a new commandment
That you love one another
Just as I have loved you
You also love one another
And because you love one another
Everyone will recognize you
As my disciples

THE GOSPEL OF JOHN, CHAPTER 13

CONTENTS

(Songs and final poem in *italics*)

The Child	11
Magdalene	14
St John in Gloucestershire	16
Cup	18
Like this	19
Cathar	20
White Cherry	21
This Time	22
Seek not to hold her	24
La Source	25
For Valentine's Day	27
People of the Earth	28
The Language of the Mother	30
Paracelsus	31
Achilles Heel	33
For a Real Poet	35
Shaman	36
Burning River	38
Summer	39
St Jean du Puy	40
Triune	42
The Tree of Mary	44
Mary	46
Vertical Wall	47
Birth of the Eagle	49
Blue Room	51
Cherry Blossom III	53
Pathway with a Heart	54
Unicorn	56
The Summer is Come	58

Strawberries & Cream	59
No Walls	61
Tympanum	62
Roses in the Subways	63
Assignment	65
She who Bears the Future	67
Snow	69
Lament for the Lily	70
Stubble Burning	72
Cocoon	74
Crossback Spider	76
It has to be Love	78
Soil	79
Let the Centre Hold	81
On Dursley Ridge	82
Prayer for Winter	84
Ballad of the Woman in Green	86
Listen	88
Wild Man	89
I do not touch you	91
Blueness	93
These Latter Days	95
Under the White Cherry	98
Vierge Noire	100
Rose in Deep Water	101
Resurrection	103
Gratitude	105
Initiation	106
You are the pain behind my heart	107

The Child

Who *is* this child
born across the threshold of the year
naked and wordless
whose coming is disguised in tinsel
concealed and cancelled out of consciousness
in multicoloured fog and glitz
carolled round and round this
carousel of hollow horses
days galloping nowhere . . .
up and down
up and down?

Who *is* this child
born in the tightest moment he could find
open and defenceless
whose face is invisible through windows
where Midas rules in splendour
turning every bauble over
to golden gold golden
laughing while he has forgotten
forgotten what he has forgotten
forgotten that he has not eaten
today nor yesterday, not eaten
not to his *heart's* content?

Who *is* this child
spoken unspeaking
from out of my unspeakable darkness;
naked and wordless
open defenceless
with nothing
nothing but wisps
of straw for bedding
not even words to wrap him in?

Who *is* this child
conceived in reverence
into the epitome of darkness
newer than this moment here
which never was and never will be
whom I love as only a mother can
retiring into myself in wonder
at his aloneness
at his lone and radiant one-ness?

Do you recognize him now, this stranger,
strange because new, newcomer?
You are he is you
none other
naked as you are and lonely
cold in this midwinter stable
under cover of my darkness
without even a word to warm you . . .
excepting one to name yourself with
so slight a word to make a garment
but it is *all* and *everything*:
I AM
the name you have re-membered
the shaft of light which made you
the shaft which set my shadows reeling.

And this place here?
This is Bethlehem.
Here where the pepsi cans are rolling
and the chip shop queue is growing.
and winter prunus glows in gardens
and they collect for suffering creatures
and the streets are full of friends
and shoppers and buskers and jugglers and children
and friends and people to meet and people to
smile with

and someone sticks swastikas
on the lampposts (calling for
white power and hanging)
for where there is light
there also is darkness;
here where the westering sun is a glory
over the farthest of these five hills
smiling between the beacon and the barrow
bright burnishing the winding holy river.

This place here
where *you* are born
naked single and alone . . .
this is Bethlehem
where everything begins.

Magdalene

In the dark of my moon
at the blood sacrifice
I conceived the spirit

Knowing not a man
yet knew I the Man

Cup to the sun I became
chalice to the unborn light
round bellied lute
bearing, resonant and mute
the unsung harmony
of the singing spheres

From the root of my being
upwards, I was
only vessel
only womb
swept clear as white crystal
by the wind of the
divine word

Under the arching roof of the temple
in seven chapels
lovely as the calyx of
the rose
in sacred silence
I received the
divine sword

And from the dark of her womb
the earth trembled
with hope
and helplessness

Now wherever she waits
for the seed to surge
there, in her crypts,
she hides me.

Open my dark gates
O my deliverer
for the seed has come
full term
In the rush and flow of time
take gently into your strong hands
the second generation
and sing him abroad
on the fair wind,
out of your heart, as
love.

St John in Gloucestershire

Oh, the poppy is a burning word
that blooms on every corner;
and your voice is a single standing stone
that points to high midsummer;
and butterflies are your two eyes
settled restless on the vetches.
I'm afraid of the shade in the midsummer sun
and all the dreams it catches.
Your feet are charred by the hot high road
while the rose flames on the briar—
'I'll take you over now,' you said,
'I'll take you over the fire.'

Forty days in the wilderness
in the high green woods of Dursley.
The Earth was alive on the dragon's road
from Cam to Leonard Stanley.
On Robinswood you grew wide wings
to sail over Severn reaches;
settled down on the crown of Cooper's Hill
above the tallest beeches.
Then up to the rim of Cotteswold
when the sun could rise no higher—
'I'll take you over now,' you said,
'I'll take you over the fire.'

Oh, the daisy looked you in the eye,
saying, 'Tell me, are you ready?'
And the tottergrass trembled as you passed
saying 'Can you hold it steady?'
And the lark on the shoulder of Cotteswold
sang, 'Can you fly as I do?'
And the Elkstone bell called as it rang,
'Can you sound as far as I do?'
And your feet were charred by the hot high road
and torn by the twisting briar—

'I'll take you over now,' you said,
'I'll take you over the fire.'

You plumbed the depths on Painswick Hill
where the green sward lies inviting,
and you paced the streets of Gloucester town
where the sightless crowds were passing;
and then you roamed down Severn's banks
where the poppies bloom in summer,
and the mud flats crack in the midday sun
at the bending of the river;
then you waded into the salt brown tide
of Severn's holy water—
'I'll take you over now,' you said,
'I'll take you over the fire.'

Cup

Opaque and foam white
This body lies
At the moment where the tide meets
The land,
Beautiful as alabaster
or the sea smooth stones
Of Atlantic inlets,
Sculpted by the green wave
And the moon.

This is not mine
This vessel, which becomes translucent
As the tide rises,
And dissolves into limpid light
At the sea's edge,
Containing for an oceanic instant
The whole round world—
Before the wave breaks
And drops it once more
Out of boundlessness,
Onto the gull guarded gateway
Of the solid shore.

This is not mine
This quintessence of frozen flow.
It is earth's daughter, it is
The cup I carry and
The cup that carries me,
Lent to my seeking soul
For a span
To catch the sun and tide of
Transmutation,
To bring forth out of irridescence
The son,
In showers of gold-glistening
Transparent
Blood.

Like this

I always dreamed of starways and hidden doorways
But I didn't know the stars were inside my heart.
I was always fond of flying, I could do it without trying,
But that was before the sky opened up inside.
That was before you sailed up on my shore,
So easily riding the storm,
And before you there was no door—
There was no doorway inwards.
I didn't see the steps to ground me;
I couldn't feel the love around me.
I didn't know I could feel so happy
And I never knew, I never knew,
I never knew it could be like this.

There is nothing much to choose, between habits and evasions;
Ratrun or escape route—it's all much the same.
When there's only half a candle, maybe lifetimes to untangle,
It's easier to play the old familiar games.
That was before you rose up in my path,
Splitting the illusions apart,
'Til the light was spilling out of my heart.
You were my doorway inwards.
Now when I feel your love surround me
Then I can touch the earth inside me.
I didn't know I could feel so happy
And I never knew, I never knew,
I never knew it could be like this.

That was before you rose up in my path,
Splitting the illusions apart,
'Til the light was spilling out of my heart.
You were my doorway inwards.
Now when I feel your love surround me
Then I can touch the earth inside me.
I didn't know I could feel so happy
And I never knew, I never knew,
I never knew it could be like this.

Cathar

Let me not escape from this moment:
Keep me captive in your arms until I see
From under the wrinkled, earthen lids of time
The sudden eye of love wink blindingly;
And all that ever blossomed, blossom now,
Radiant white along the blackened bough.

White Cherry

The white cherry blossom haunts me,
mocking my fears
with hints of some greater purity
beyond experience.

Facing you I feel naked.
No, not unclothed, but naked
nonetheless.
The roles we so often wear, when we meet,
were left somewhere,
superfluous, both yours and mine;
and there is nothing held between
except our masks, which emphasize
and do not disguise.

I will slip into this green current,
entrusting self and safety
to the muscular flow,
letting the alder trimmed world
            slide
        gracefully
backwater.

Who knows whither
the glistening river sings,
and whether and where,
at the next landfall,
        the white cherry blooms?

This Time

I came out onto the marble steps
And I knew that you had gone,
Though the sun didn't seem to have moved at all
Where he stood at the height of noon;
And I saw your cat sitting tall and strange
In the dust of that final day;
And he looked at me with his golden eyes
And then he walked away—
But this time we've got to get it right.

I didn't mean to let you down.
I was just too young to see,
And simply too small to understand
The trust you had placed in me;
So I packed my bags and took to the road
In the teeth of the rising storm,
And cities were drowned and washed away
And the olden days were gone—
But this time we've got to get it right.

The path was dark and overgrown;
There were shadows at every turn,
And I seemed to be walking for centuries
And my limbs and my heart were torn;
But just when I'd given up every hope,
So numb I could scarcely stand,
A wise little man with a face of earth
Came and took my trembling hand,
Saying, 'This time we're going to get it right'.

Before my feet the silver path
Shone white with a silver sheen,
Straight to the heart of a mystery
In the light of the rising moon;
And I passed through a thousand deaths and births
And yet they were only one;
And now we are standing face to face

And a new world has begun—
And this time we're going to get it right.

I didn't mean to let you down
I was just too young to see
And simply too small to understand
The trust you had placed in me;
But now we've been given another chance
And the cat is here to stay.
As he looks at me with his golden eyes
I know he won't go away.
And this time we're going to get it right.

Seek not to hold her

Seek not to hold her
for she is given
to the bees.

Her breasts are two
white roses
dispensing sweet nectar

and the ripening fruit
of her womb is what the world
waits for—
in the patient eyes
of her lover
and in the flaming palms
of supplicants
starving, under the Indian
sun.

Seek not to hold her
for she will give birth
among the bees, alone
in the wilderness

and when she passes
wide winged
with her precious progeny—
on the windswept soil
which has forgotten
how to weep
you will hear the
fresh dew falling.

La Source

Secret de la source, si bien cachée sous les rochers:
Secret des paroles, paroles de ma bien aimée.

Elle est assise sous les amandiers fleuris,
Toujours silencieuse, toujours elle se taît:
Et quand elle ne me parle, c'est une source muette et tarie,
Tandis que le pays devient désert, et mon coeur tout déséché.

Secret de la source si bien cachée sous les rochers:
Secret des paroles, paroles de ma bien aimée.

Elle regarde s'envoler la fumée
Des feux parmi les vignes, où brûlent les branches coupées,
Et quand elle ne me parle, c'est un arbre sans oiseaux,
Tandis que mon coeur devient assoifé
Du chant joyeux de l'eau.

Secret de la source si bien cachée sous les rochers:
Secret des paroles, paroles de ma bien aimée.

Là bas sur les terrasses, j'irai me promener
Et si je trouve courage, alors je lui dirai
La douleur de mon coeur souffrant, qui chez elle voudrait rentrer,
Les épines de silence, qui poussent sur son rosier.

Secret de la source si bien cachée sous les rochers:
Secret des paroles, paroles de ma bien aimée.

Et si elle se retourne, me regardant de ses beaux yeux gris,
La brume du matin par le soleil sera percée;
Et si elle me parle, mon coeur en soupirera
Et j'aurai de l'espoir qu'en bon échange, son coeur elle me donnera.

Secret de la source si bien cachée sous les rochers:
Secret des paroles, paroles de ma bien aimée.

Et lorsqu'elle me parle, les ruisseaux vont couler,
Nourris par la source, sortie de son rocher;
Et lorsqu'elle me parle, mon coeur sera raffraîchi
Et partout dans la campagne assoifée fleuriront les cerisiers.

Secret de la source si bien cachée sous les rochers:
Secret des paroles, paroles de ma bien aimée.

Lorsque coule la source, loin du vacarme des cités,
Entre souvenir et avenir le lien sera renoué;
Et j'écoute dans la source le chant trop longtemps manqué
Et je sais que je serai uni, uni avec ma bien aimée.

Secret de la source si bien cachée sous les rochers:
Secret des paroles, paroles de ma bien aimée.

For Valentine's Day

The grass is shot with crocus gold
and healing mauve, born of gladness and the Mother
and there will be daffodils in throngs, my love,
under the sycamores.

It will be a spring beyond all imagining,
borne in on the mating calls of doves
under brown eaves, and oblivious of
buses and the busy roads, of
rigidity and railings and
petty failings.

It surges through your fingers and toes, freeing
green coils of growth and
flows of flowers
lighting up our hearts, up from their
sevenfold hermetic sleep.

Pluto plots in the dark, among fears and
cowerings, tears and lowering winter fog.
But if you did not know his deeps,
how could you greet the spring and our
new grown love,
and celebrate with well-strung heart
the return of song?

People of the Earth

We are the people of the earth.

Our kinfolks are the dogwood and the maple,
The hickory and the pine our brothers too,
And our footfalls leave no traces
Across the secret places
And we know where the deer and beaver go.

We climb the mountain trails in the morning,
To greet the sun arising in the east,
And to hear the little birds
Singing praises without words,
For the life that springs in every feathered breast.

And we watch the Dog Star rising in the evening
And we understand the voices of the trees,
And the song the river sings
And the swish of eagles' wings—
There is language to be heard in every breeze.

But now you come to ravage and to plunder
And to rape the darkness of your mother's womb.
You destroy our holy mountains
With no reckoning nor accounting
How you turn her living body to the tomb.

And you use her bones for fuel to make power
That can burn and poison every living thing,
Bringing sickness, death and sorrow
And more to come tomorrow—
Could be soon there will be nothing left to sing.

O, put your feet down gentle on the mountain,
O, put your feet down gentle on the earth;
For you know she is your mother
And there'll never be another
To sustain you every moment from your birth.

We are the keepers of the earth;
We guard her hidden gateways to the dawn,
In the silence of her shadows,
On her bluffs and in her hollows,
Until the day of brotherhood shall come.

We are the people of the earth.

The Language of the Mother

Malleret

It is time to learn the language
of the Mother.

Unroll in Merlin's catalytic classes
where, among wet rocks and summer's withered grasses,
you may learn the vocabulary of mosses,
and where each particular cloud drop,
suspended on the misted hazel twig,
reflects in diamond-studded detail
the flickering words
apprehended in your moist roots, where
everything begins.

Grasp the grammar of your five limbs
and, when the gleam in your lover's eye pierces
the veils you wear for your protection,
trust the subtle rippling of
moondust along the pathways of your
resurrecting body.

She speaks here
where we stand enraptured, in this abandoned
upper room
among bird droppings and
faded domestic memories . . .
She speaks
and we descend the dusty stairs, to listen
before the empty hearth.
but we do not yet understand
the words for 'kindling' and 'brand'.

It is time to learn the language
of the Mother.

And Merlin waits for us without,
in the dank November twilight,
among his rain drenched
dictionaries.

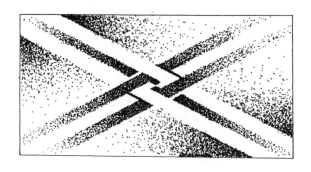

Paracelsus

Lean away from all learning
like this bent alder
determined to ignore the
vertical road to heaven
trailing twigs in the eddies
and songs of life
and playing bridge to the nimble-heeled
perch to the trout fisher
and mother to the gold-spiked moss

My roots will find no purchase
in books or the teachings of sages
I am at the mutating tip of species
where rhizome becomes foot
and fares forth over the speckled rock
restless for the river

Metanoia!
cries the gaunt bird of the wilderness
losing his loneliness in ecstasy—
and crystals
remembering the wide splendour of rainbows
shoot out of the deep earth
in showers of amethyst, rose and incandescent light

'These are my eldest children
in whom I am well pleased!'
the Mother sings
as they spread peacock wings
and disperse over the city
where upturned eyes
in wakening surprise
wonder
who tampered with the lights
these Christmas nights
over the Jardin des Plantes

But it was only you and I
taking our feet out of the clay for a moment
and burning the old books
on the market square

Achilles Heel

You have hoisted up the red rag
The red rag to the bull,
And now the horns are lowered
To move in for the kill.
You have got more than you bargained for
When you let that arrow fly,
As the blood drips down from his shoulder wound
Under the bleeding sky.
Tell me, why did you come barefoot to this ground?

You have truly flung the gauntlet.
All is fair in love and war.
I read you in the cloudshapes,
I read you loud and clear.
If this is the time for duelling
Then I'm ready for the fray.
I can feel the smart where you hit my heart
The day before yesterday.
Tell me, why did you come barefoot to this ground?

There are some who would call it shifty
And some just shifting shape,
That you have grown a single horn
To pierce me in the neck.
But if you have grown a single horn
Then I shall grow me two,
And you will find that I am not kind
But sure of what I do.
Tell me, why did you come barefoot to this ground?

You have hoisted up the red rag
Under the darkening sky.
If you have shown no mercy
Then neither shall I.
If you expose your Achilles heel
Don't say I didn't warn,
As the wounded beast lowers his great crest

Curved like the sickle moon.
Tell me, why did you come barefoot to this ground?

They have come down from the vineyards
They have come up from the sea;
Taken seats in the arena,
To watch the battle fly;
And some will back the one-horned beast
And some will back the two.
They will shed no tears for the wasted years
If one of us should go.
Tell me, why did you come barefoot to this ground?

I don't really want to hurt you,
But there is nothing else to do.
If you lay down the challenge
Can I just let it go?
For we have to face the wild beast.
Can either of us win?
If both are slain, can we survive that pain
And be born to try again?
Tell me, why did you come barefoot to this ground?

For a Real Poet

Your body is warmer
than when last
we met,
as if you had let the
words penetrate
deeper into your substance,
in-forming it,
not afraid to let
Beauty nest there.

But I could not watch you,
bending with the words
as you spoke,
having to tend to my own space,
as they entered
on flaming wings.

Such words are my
aspiration . . .
and from the dark vortex
below my foundations,
melody spirals up
to meet them.

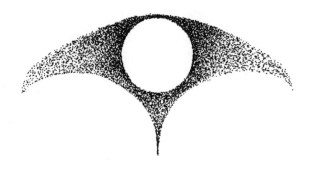

Shaman

This man is a dancer
among stones,
a shepherd of the
inanimate.
Like eagle's feathers
his curved fingers caress
the wind
and where he walks, the earth flames
with desire—

desire to awaken
in chalk chasms and chines
in tumbled rock temples
and under the pale breast
of the winter bare hill.

Where he sits among roots,
becoming soil and clay,
so still,
the trees pull free to peer
over his shoulder
at the tall strangers who circle
around his heart.

This man of no name
turns a slow deliberate spiral
on the rock where, for aeons,
the rain has wept channels full
of feathered ferns and lichens;

and deep below, I watch in wonder
a white ball of brilliance grow
and thread far unerring paths of healing,
clear through wet stone and winter bough.

He turns—
and above the dance the hawk hangs,
for an instant oblivious of prey,
poised,
a perfect master of the
rising day.

Burning River

I must be going, no longer staying;
The burning Thames I have to cross—
But I will be guided without a stumble
Into the arms of my own true love.

And if I stumble it was I that planted
The crooked stone that I stumble on,
And should I fall I will rise again, love;
No halt nor danger that can hold me in.

It broke my heart when first we parted,
When you took the stony road down to the sea,
When you turned away, love, to face the ocean
And bitter were the words you left with me.

In the fires of war we have consumed each other;
We have torn each other limb from limb:
No pain too eager, no knife nor dagger
Too sharp to draw the crimson blood again.

You were the black bull and I the dancer,
You were the hunter, I was on the run;
You were the salmon hooked and I the angler,
I the soldier shot and you the gun.

Now the path grows narrow and hard to follow,
High walls of steel and stone shut out the sun,
And the river burns where I must cross over
To reach your heart and your arms again.

I must be going, no longer staying
The burning Thames I have to cross—
But I will be guided without a stumble
Into the arms that I love the best.

And if I stumble it was I that planted
The crooked stone that I stumble on,
And should I fall I will rise again, love,
And if I should fall I will rise again.

Summer

When the sun calls
I uproot, uprush,
fingers diaphanous dandy down,
dangling body
no bigger than silver-held
seeds, alight in the sundrift,
torn skywards on a pale wind,
headfirst, all ear and longing
for out there, where you just might be
somewhere, hovering.

But she, this tree
another me, inverted,
clings head downwards to the light within,
below her far flung filigree hair
roots and, knowing the Mother's
sheer and dauntless love
spreads her limbs upwards
greenskirted and mysterious
hung with silken hairs and june scented
shimmerings,
enticing you down
with a seamless certainty . . .

and you respond, yes,
sudden and silver shafted
scattering stars . . . and she
endows the air, in gratitude.

St Jean du Puy

J'ai quitté le val ou poussent les oliviers
Aux racines enlacées,
Dont les feuilles agitées par la bise
Ont la couleur de fumée.

[REFRAIN:
Car c'est un rêve de feu qui m'anime
De tes yeux embrasés,
De ta voix qui perce comme un éclair
Et résonne dans la vallée.]

J'ai traversé les vignes qui dansent
Les bras levés vers le soleil.
Je suis venu au pays des roches nues et blanches
Comme une épaule de femme.

REFRAIN

J'ai roulé devant les grands panneaux bleus
Qui annoncent le fracas des villes;
Mais je n'avais pas affaire dans les grands boulevards,
Le long des trottoirs imbéciles.

REFRAIN

Parmi les montagnes enceintes
Je suis monté sur ton puy blanc,
Gardien de tes pensées, site de tes fêtes
Puissant de ton oraison.

REFRAIN

Là ou tu planes puissant comme un aigle
Au dessus de la terre endormie,
Je suis venu chercher ton baptême
Et un trésor secret et sans prix.

REFRAIN

Ce trésor enfoui parmi les chênes
C'est le chant de ton coeur,
Qui toujours aime et se donne
A l'âme vivant de la terre.

REFRAIN

Car c'est une parole de feu qui t'anime,
Rhythme sans cesse prononcé,
Parole de changement et de métamorphose,
Qui résonne par toute la vie,
Et dont je ne veux m'échapper.

Triune

Under the light of the countenance
I sat within the body of
the man.
In that body was a stillness expanding,
a loosening, a straightening,
as of a sunray settling
on snow,
a brightening bell round sound,
a vibrant quickening, quick silver glistening,
a listening.

Onto that head, held in still awakening,
came many crowns, light livening
or brow chastening;
upreared head of cobra, diadem,
tooled gold ornate of jewelling,
cool circlets of silver, into pale mist hastening
and vanishing.

Within that body I was woman
form giving and form given
called into colours by his waiting—
(impersonal, personal, all knowing
all things expecting, none needing).
Within that body I became,
am still becoming.   I am
womb of waters . . .
womb-man.

Within that heart of hallows,
holy hollow,
there was a flowering,
first pin prick pulsing,
into full bloom burgeoning,
into all light widening,
brightening, unconcealing—

sungold child revealing;
Within that child white bird descending.

And back again the journey taking:
spirit bird, white feathers shaking,
nestling in the heart of hallows,
womb-man, woman, form redeeming,
in a robe of clear light gleaming,
from within new song receiving.
In the body of the Father
Christ is son and bride together.
I dreamed a bird,
Child, master, healer.

The Tree of Mary

Oh, the cedar made the cross of death;
The thorn tree made the crown;
The olive a cup to catch the blood,
That from the cross ran down;
But of all the trees in the tall green wood,
The beech is dear to me;
And dear she is, for in the seed
She sings the song of three.
Rejoice and sing the song of three.

The oak tree built the fishing boats;
The rod of birch was made;
The ash both smooth and light did make
The spear that pierced his side;
But of all the trees in the forest tall,
The beech is dear to me;
And dear she is, for in the seed
She sings the song of three.
Rejoice and sing the song of three.

Three for the goddess let us sing,
Of mother, maid and crone,
Of earth in travail bringing forth
The god of love reborn.
The beech she knows the moment well
When thou reborn shalt be;
She knows it well, for in her roots
A candle burns for thee.
Rejoice and sing the song of three.

Three for Solomon king and she
Who was to be his queen;
And for him who built the ark of gold,
A secret all unseen.
Of all the trees the beech she knows
How the temple healed will be:
She knows it well, for in the seed

She sings the song of three.
Rejoice and sing the song of three.

Three for father, mother, son,
The holy family;
For the shaft of gold that pierced the earth
At the first nativity.
We praise and sing the holy womb
The third of the trinity.
The beech the tree of Mary is
For she sings the song of three.
Rejoice and sing the song of three.

Mary stands between two beasts
And she is the queen of light,
And she loves their fierce and flaming gaze
Beside the inward gate.
The beech the tree of Mary is
Whose child reborn shall be,
And dear she is, for in the seed
She sings the song of three.
Rejoice and sing the song of three.

Mary

My body's the boat that will bring you to shore
My life is the mast and my deed is the oar
My songs are the sails and my soul is the wind
And my words are the swift birds before and behind
All my being is nothing but vessel for thee
May the tale of thy coming be spoken through me

Vertical Wall

It was a slow moving crawl,
climbling that vertical wall,
holding on by my fingernails,
couldn't look down below.
Now I know you weren't there
I didn't get anywhere—
I've grown wings on my shoulder blades . . .
I'm letting go.

Whether you come when I call
or pick me up when I fall,
it doesn't matter at all—
you're always here.

She's in a moon daisy daze,
in a Whitsunday haze,
in her cow parsley petticoats,
in a dream the earth lies;
whilst the tiny brown beads,
floating dandelion seeds
on their featherdown parachutes,
burrow into her thighs.

Whether you come when I call
or pick me up when I fall,
it doesn't matter at all—
you're always here.

There is a white tongue of flame
and a lark singing your name,
and a pair of blue butterflies,
as they dance round my head;
and if I lie very still
on this magical hill,
then a whole new dimension grows—
only give me the Word.

Whether you come when I call
or pick me up when I fall,
it doesn't matter at all—
you're always here.

It was a slow-moving crawl
climbing that vertical wall,
holding on by my fingernails,
couldn't look down below.
Now I know you weren't there,
I didn't get anywhere—
I've grown wings on my shoulder blades . . .
I'm letting go.

Whether you come when I call,
or pick me up when I fall,
it doesn't matter at all—
you're always here;
whether you come when I call
or pick me up when I fall,
it doesn't matter at all—
you're always here.

Birth of the Eagle

The earth was warm to his feet—
outcrops of white rock, smoothed
and shaped by the chiselling centuries,
thyme caught in crevices,
aromatic with memories.
He listened to the language of the oak,
old, told in fragments and
short phrases, caught by the limbs
and not the mind.
Climbing, he rose within his body
shook dark wings out of his shoulders
settled russet feathers fanwise about a
strong neck, and,
feeling the throb of familiar music
caressing his feet,
curled talons
to clasp
the mounting recognition.

Suddenly he *was* . . .
exploding into the arms of the sun
in a white heat of anguish—
memory uprushing into a wild
feathering of pinions,
fierce curve of beak
echoing white slope of rock,
eyes shimmering with mountain clarity—
golden.
Here on this high and sunbright tower he *was*
the wind at rest.

Beneath that gaze in a gilded haze
I lay, an open book, wherein he read
each wrinkle and each line
gouged by the hands of men,
every careful scratch of the sure and dread
march of heaving conquest and rapine—
my crucifixion, in deep tones and colours done,
and beholding my living death,
his birth began.

Blue Room

Here,
in this blue room,
we are spiralling down.

Here,
in this blue room,
there's a journey to make,
don't try to escape—
there is light some where.

Here,
in this blue room,
we are spiralling down.

Here,
in this blue room,
let me take off your coat
tread it under your feet—
you won't be needing it now;

For you'll be light,
travelling light,
travelling,
travelling light,
you will be light,
travelling.

Here,
in this blue room,
we are fast free falling.

Here,
in this blue room,
there's a creature with horns,
but it's only a mask,
I've often seen it before.

Here,
in this blue room,
we are inside outside.

Here,
in this blue room,
there is no-one but me;
you can take off your mask—
you won't be needing it now;

For you'll be light,
travelling light,
travelling,
travelling light,
you will be light,
travelling.

And we won't even take a lunch hour break
and the man you were meeting at six can wait
and I'm holding this moment 'til it fills up the sky
'til your heart cracks
and the light spills
out onto my hands—

Then you'll be light,
travelling light,
travelling light,
travelling light,
travelling,
travelling light,
you will be light,
travelling.

Cherry Blossom III

Every year
everywhere in gardens
and along the river   the cherry blossom
cleaves a clean pathway
into my heart
a white wound blooming under
the keen blade of spring

This is the purity
beyond experience
releasing white blood in
petals of light

My heart is spreadeagled
wide to this celebration of whiteness
witness of this celebration
my heart is the white bird you shot
from amongst the cherry blossom

I remember your shoulders
tensed with aiming

I remember the white blood
flowering

Every year again
the cherry blossom
in gardens
blade sharp   again
and again

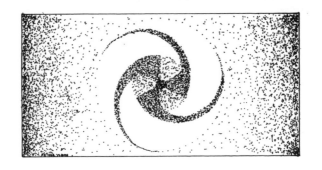

Pathway with a Heart

It was a good book they gave to me,
But what's the use if I can't see
   to turn the pages over?
All those lost dreams of yesterday—
Tears in my eyes make me forget
   I chose to be a rover.
Not for me the beaten track, no,
   Not the well worn phrases.
I choose a pathway with a heart—
   No stones to mark the stages.

Another way might look the same,
But there's only pain and an aching soul
   for those that walk along it;
But mine is a pathway with a heart,
Which calls to me and makes me sing,
   whenever I walk upon it.
Not for me the printed word,
   No gurus and no sages.
I choose a pathway with a heart—
   No familiar stopping places.

Though each of us is all alone,
It's strange that I expect to see you
just round every corner.
I let you go and yet I know,
The more I do, the more our pathways
seem to be coming closer:
Near is far and far is near,
No well known destination.
If you choose a pathway with a heart,
The goal is your own creation.

Though each of us is all alone,
It's strange that I expect to see you
just round every corner.
I let you go and yet I know,
The more I do, the more our pathways
seem to be coming closer,
closer . . .
closer.

Unicorn

Steep flanked, splay legged
he is, and angular
tottering along the
high boundary between dream
and waking, unwary of
the drop—
small nostrils flaring the unfamiliar
atmosphere of shift and sheer fall
where imaginations coalesce,
compact and sweep down into unsuspecting
matter.

He is white and
soft as the white peony in summer
new opened under the fingers of the
sun,
the tiny, fabled horn a bud merely
upheld proudly on the small round
brow.

He is new and shining.
The white brilliance of his dawning
conceals the shadowed gateway of his birthing.

This is my child
born out of aching chasms
of moist stalagmitred splendour
beneath my belly of hot white stone
scantily concealed by sun dried grass and
pungent thyme and the ubiquitous murmur
of winged things
where once you lay and did not
see my face, nor feel my trembling
under the sharp, dark
juniper.

He is new and shining
The white brilliance of his dawning
conceals the shadowed gateway of his birthing,
while small hooves cleave the jagged fringes of
your discreet days
threatening dimensions you are afraid to dream of.

But you do not see his mother—
for I lie shadowed under your own
limbs, curled about your belly in
invisible embrace
and every thought shed carelessly is
potent in the pathways
of my subterrestrial womb
to be bodied forth at last
on that high narrow ridge of
dreamfall, where now he
stands

Smooth flanked he is, the Unicorn,
strong and rapid of growth
deadly of horn
cleaving the clouds of your unknowing
with the first bolts of storm
in the high stillness of approaching solstice

Will you turn again and learn?

Behold the heavy brooding of my gates
and, before he turns upon you
the fury of his purity,
take on and own this untamed master
of the occult heart, and
recognizing me, behold

your son

The Summer's Come

'The summer is come
and I know not whence it came'
Paracelsus

At last the rose unfolds
full and sweet
redeeming the thorn

This pure redness
can no longer be contained
bursting across the thick air between
which casts us outcast
each in a lonely cavity
of skin.

The rose glows
rapid fire along a high cable
crimson affirmation
co-mingling of hearts.

The rose is master mason of the
inward gate

and within
the centre and the wild peripherous world
are one
begetting healing,
a fragrance lingering,
lilt of a white feather
at every verge and boundary

The summer is come—master
Out of thy heart it came.
Thy heart, master?
Or was it mine?

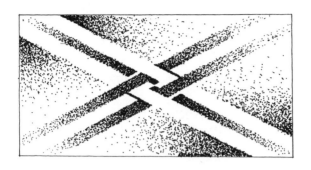

Strawberries & Cream

Here at this empty table
You drop your head onto your arms
afraid of losing what you never had
afraid to see what is within your grasp.

I am both here and not here
I come to meet me from all directions.

You, as other
are the cream on the strawberries
indigestible and superfluous
whatever my desires.

I grow you from inside me
gathering you about me
as the sprouting seed
gathers leaves from the periphery,

and suddenly
this wet summer of many sorrows
unfolds you full blown and life size
in my garden

but the paradise of soft kisses
is an illusion
unless *you* are both here and
not here
unless *you* come to meet *you*
from all directions

unless *you* unfold *me* from
inside you
ingathering from the four wise winds
this warm and aching body
trembling with your hidden life.

Endow me with your name
and I shall give you
my gentle death.
There are strawberries
on the table,
and cream
in a little jug.

No Walls

Don't bar the door into your garden,
Don't shut the gate with lock and key.
I long to touch the summer roses
And smell the thyme and rosemary.

If the door seems locked into my garden
Then in your hand you hold the key.
Come in and touch the summer roses
And smell the thyme and rosemary.

Oh I can feel it from a distance,
Whenever you turn your face away,
Giving your smiles to another
And keeping only the tears for me.

I will not turn by back upon you,
Nor will I keep my smiles apart,
And my tears are drops of silver water
To feed the courage of your heart.

Sometimes I think the sky is raining
And the wind is only cold for me,
And I can feel my courage waning,
It takes all my strength to lift my feet.

You are the sky that is always raining;
You are the wind that chills your limbs;
Yours are the clouds that hide the sunlight
And you are the space where love begins.

There's a butterfly upon my window
Just hatching out from his cocoon.
His wings expand to catch the sunlight,
The clearest colours I've ever seen.

You are the butterfly emerging,
Spreading your wings out to the sun.
There are no walls around the garden
And the thyme has just begun to bloom.

Tympanum

(The Troubadour)

I am not any thing you give a name to,
There is nothing I am bound to do;
I stand within the circle of my freedom;
There is nowhere I am bound to go;

But if you should wish to circumscribe me,
Bend your thinking round into an O,
Stretching the finest skin across it,
Tightened like the drawn string on a bow.

I am nothing but an instrument of hearing,
A membrane, taut as ever any drum,
All senses fused together to make one.

Strike me with your name and with your beauty;
Vibrating with your pain and with your love,
I shall pierce the very stars with song.

Ascension
28:5:87

Roses in the Subways

When you closed the door, love,
A rose came up in the street,
Splitting open the tarmac,
I got blood on my feet.
But your house is empty now;
You've put it up for sale.
You're going out another way, love,
Unravelling another trail.

Chorus: But it's taking over the city,
It's rambling all around the town
And you'd see roses in the subways
If only you'd turn around.

When you said goodbye, love,
I was looking at cloudy skies:
No light on your brow,
And no stars in your eyes.
Oh but the thorns were hard and sharp,
Though you couldn't see them grow,
And the road was cracking right across, love;
That rose was pushing through.

Chorus: And it's taking over the city,
It's rambling all around the town
And you'd see roses in the subways
If only you'd turn around.

I know there are many ways—
You can travel by bus or plane
And you can drive the same highway,
Just moving in a different lane;
But something's happening out here now,
Just as you turn to go:
The earth is bleeding roses, love,
And I only want you to know.

Chorus: *For they're taking over the city,*
They're rambling all around the town
And you'd see roses in the subways
If only you'd turn around,
If only you'd turn around.

Assignment

They gave to me my orders.
They told me it would be hard.
They told me you'd forgotten your origins,
You would just be a face in the crowd.
Maybe you don't even know your name,
Let alone the reason why you came,
But it's written in my heart
In letters of flame:
My assignment is you,
My assignment is you,
My assignment is you.

I started in the city,
In the crowds in the rush hour trains,
In the places people go to be silent
To escape from the storms and the rain.
Wherever I look there are faces to love,
And love is the only real clue I have,
But to find you I know that it's more than enough.
My assignment is you,
My assignment is you,
My assignment is you.

When you landed you had the freedom
To remember or to forget.
You could flood the world with light
Every step you take,
You could make the earth move,
Every word you speak,
And peace would grow like roses
Under your hand,
And peace would grow like roses
Under your hand.

They gave to me my orders.
They told me I had to sing,
To remind you of what you intended,

To remind you of where you began.
One of these days we shall meet again.
If I sing it to you will you know your name?
For it's written in my heart
In letters of flame:
My assignment is you,
My assignment is you,
My assignment is you.

She who Bears the Future

It is autumn   and
I am pregnant again
but this time it is with you
with you
How surprised you would be
thinking yourself mature
ordered
separate

Your curled head rests
against my pubis
settled gently
like gold leaves on the earth

To be this close
with you
is as joyful as
cupping the first warmly shining
conker in my palm
an irresistible joy   ripe
and rippling

Sometimes I smile to think
you are there
nestled in this slim body
so real I can feel
no see
where your feet
importune the ribs under my heart

But no-one knows
and I become younger daily
reaching a new virginity
haloed with laughter
a sure-footed purity
practical
with no pious pretensions

Truly
it will be a
virgin birth

Snow

grave cloth or
birth linen
or unsullied belly, strange
and pure, tufted with misted pine,
where everything sleeps
but this little stream,
steep, warm gash
in the white

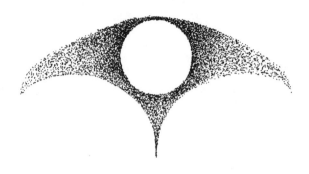

Lament for the Lily

*Cold blow the winds out of the north
And winter's coming early.
Cold blow the winds out of the north
And winter's coming early.
Heavy falls the bitter rain,
Arrows loaded with our pain
And cold the shafts come sweeping in,
Threatening the lily.*

*Where is the king for whom she wakes,
Waiting late and early?
Where is the king for whom she wakes,
Waiting late and early?
The winter curls about his throne
And all her champions are gone
And the sun pales as he looks upon
The bruising of the lily.*

*The armies roll, harsh to a man,
Spread over her body, take what they can.
Lawless rules the greedy horde,
'Line my pockets, then hit the road'.*

*The armies roll, harsh to a man,
Spread over her body, take what they can.
Lawless rules the greedy horde,
'Line my pockets, then hit the road'.*

White as the snow her body lies,
More beautiful than any;
White as the snow her body lies,
More beautiful than any.
Does she live still, does she breathe?
Can she still awake to love?
My heart bleeds when I'm thinking of
The raping of the lily.

Does she live still, does she breathe?
Can she still awake to love?
My heart bleeds when I'm thinking of
The raping of the lily.

Stubble Burning

A thin coil of smoke
still plumes skywards
from yesterday's garden fire,
conflagration of thistle and nipplewort
and the winding bindweed.

A thin skein of words
lies still on still autumn air;
weblike, tangled, uncarded,
unguarded, inchoate utterings
last sputterings of the fire you lit
in the strait gate of my furrow,
and tended, in inexorable burning lines
across my belly
taking all: weed and stubble,
joy and trouble, mousehome
and birdthorn
singeing the trees that were my bed cover.
Was ever such a lover?
The burning bridegroom
with pitchfork and firestick
claiming compensation
for the dead bride.

But I am not dead.

How should you think so?
when my heat is deeper than ever share ploughed to,
and what fires will one day leap to your harrowings
when there's an end to compensations
could drive your thinking's blunted blades
into contortions of rapid self destruction . . . or
waken the true lover who slumbers yet,
under your silent soul.

My deep fires of silver thread the brambles
dawnly with webbed light

powdering the sloes sharply with the white rime.
They promise all reawakenings and resurrections
bodily,
and body forth
the sacred fires within your blood
when it blossoms to love
beyond the barns where gloom the implements
to torture thinking and to rack
the eroded downs deep down to sow more havoc
and to harvest yet more seeds of discord.
The compensation for your burned and buried bride's
a glut of madness to sell off cheap
to the hungry.

My deep fires meditate
beyond the barns where glooms your thinking
mediating love into the long strong rays
of autumn mornings.

A thin coil of smoke grows,
gathering flame,
promising a brighter burning from below;
where words leap glowing from my deepest heart
and all the furrows burn green with them.

Cocoon

I don't know where you're going
But I know you have to go,
Because we'll never really meet until you do.
There's a kind of desolation
Trying to live with these old dreams,
When they're fraying at the edges,
And they're splitting at the seams
And a new kind of creature's showing through.

We used to share the same view,
Walk out of the same front door,
Treading barefoot on the same grass in the dew;
But our words have all dried up now
And I need to be alone,
With the frost still on the hedges
And the springtime yet to come,
Though the grey sky's beginning to turn blue.

So say goodbye; go your way—
The world is round; we'll meet again somewhere.
Leave me here in this cocoon,
While my shape is changing.

We used to face the same fears,
Stumble over the same stones,
Groping blindly through the same fog, hand in hand.
But the mist has blown away now,
There's a sharpness in the air
And the threads have snapped and broken
Of the web we used to share
And I begin to feel the circle where I stand.

I don't know where you're going
But I know you have to go,
Because we'll never really meet until you do.
There's a kind of desolation
Trying to live with these old dreams,

When they're fraying at the edges,
And they're splitting at the seams
And a new kind of creature's showing through.

So say goodbye; go your way—
The world is round; we'll meet again somewhere.
Leave me here in this cocoon,
While my shape is changing.

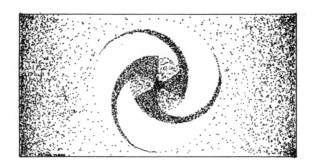

Crossback Spider

This crossback is never
at the end of its tether
because it is tethered to itself
inwardly
and there is no end to
that thread.
When the web is broken
it hangs upon the broken
thread
and drawing on that endless fine
line affixes it
with gentle kisses of its spinnerets
to the spokes of its world
and so
round and round
delicately
teasing out and touching
without amazement
until it sits
in finest rainbowed beauty
perfectly poised between the roses and
oblivious.

Sometimes I forget
the endless thread
coiled deep within
my deeps down
below where my thoughts go
felt   ready
wound upon infinity.
But drawing upon this
secret and sweet store
I could spin momently
a space in which to sit royally
all twelve senses spread
wide open to the periphery
open even to your lightest touch
knowingly.

It has to be Love

Autumn day.
The gale has scattered all the leaves away.
Emptiness.
Already thrown away my autumn dress.
And I'm curled up, hunched over,
And I'm waiting, waiting,
Waiting for the star to fall.

Might have beens—
I've discarded all my summer dreams.
It's all gone.
Nothing left except a word and a song.
And I'm a turned in, empty hollow,
And I'm waiting, waiting,
Waiting for your hand on the door.

Why do I still believe, though I've no cause to?
Still put my trust in you, though I can't feel you?
No. Only the pain.
There's only a single straw for me to cling to;
The one and only hope for me to sing to:
Love.   It has to be Love.

Autumn rain—
Tears to wash away the ache and the pain.
Longer range.
Must be ready for a weather change.
So I've let go all the anguish.
And I'm waiting, waiting,
Waiting for a break in the clouds.

Morning sun,
Forgiving all the hurt we've ever done.
Peacefulness.
A kind of balm in all the loneliness.
And I'm a deep pool, still surface,
And I'm waiting, waiting,
Still waiting for that star to fall.

Soil

This black brown stuff
which I dig in I turn over
this medium of birth
which I open with a spade
this warm smelling close smelling
matrix which I open
with my fingers folding
back the green hair
covering to plant
new things in the careful
darkness trusting
that letting the seeds go
letting the swell-bellied bulbs
go, pointing up to the sky
trusting she will know
without thought, how
to deliver them
perfumed and petal folded perfect
to the opening sun

this home of the careful worm
careful of the air and space
which it brings, digests
into this substructure
this substructure which
sticks to my fingers and
darkens my fingernails
with clean loam scents
rising from her when fingered
by the frost or drummed
on by the rain, by the
rhythms of the warm October
rain, where roots move out
exploring her with eager tenderness

and strong downward direction
thrusting into heavier deeps
of clay and stone

this deep threshold
which the plants know opens
through into light
empowering their roots, engendering
levity that can cause
rocks to split their sides
and crack open the man-made
roads in lines of laughter
that no concrete can stop
for long,
this home of fundamental levity and light
who gives birth upwards
to the sky through countless
green mouths, shaping syllables
which clothe her intimate darkness
in beauty which if we do not
admire we destroy by apathy;

this black brown stuff
which I dig in, turn over
this matrix which I open
with my fingers to plant
new things . . .
this is my body
being woman
and being woman, being she,
what to do but bear her lightness, whiteness
bear her witness
always upwards
and out, through my
green throat

Let the Centre Hold

When the new octave begins
There is a power in the wind
And the race is on to be first at the waking:
And neither party knows the names
Of this game to end all games,
And somewhere deep you know the earth is shaking:
Then let the centre hold, only let the centre hold.

When there are wings in every cloud
And I shout your name aloud,
And I know that soon there'll be an end to waiting;
When you find you are the key
To this nameless mystery,
And you begin to see the doorway I am making:
Then let the centre hold, only let the centre hold.

When the brilliance of your star
Shows me just how close you are,
Though you may have been a million light years falling;
And it may blow the world apart
When you land inside my heart,
Though the cherry blooms and all the birds are calling:
Then let the centre hold, oh please let the centre hold.

I am standing quite alone
Before a secret standing stone,
And there are faces in the mist banks of the morning;
And the last fears are all shed
From the caverns of the dead,
And along light rays of dawn I see you coming:
Then let the centre hold, oh please let the centre hold.
Let the centre hold.
Let the centre hold.

On Dursley Ridge

Swift grey skies
and the dragon mother curled
about and underneath
her monuments
breathing in and settling
into subearthly winter contemplation
in the empty opening morning

She gives us no clues:
distance and direction are
indistinct and her pathways
are slipping off the map.
She has grown lethargic
under her green cropped flanks
and the patches of purple bracken
and we must know her
only through our feet
and what wakes to
recognition on the underside
the unspoken edge
of our meeting

There are no expectations
only a knowing that
we are coming home to her
and to each other
in some higher place of soul
that she is gauge for
and measure of;
her silence pulling us up
the rutted one in fours
and drawing us in
under the roots of things

It is a privilege to sit
underneath roots, here
where the bank is hollowed out

and we can reach in
to an elemental clarity
under the grave observing
presence of trees;
and there is a tingling of forms unborn
under the surface, under my fingers,
perhaps just under these flat white stones
perhaps just under these curled beech leaves

This high monument
where the sun flashes a brief blessing
is to William Tyndale
who opened the holy books to everyman
and died for it

The revelation of mysteries
always exacts a price:
and it is her secret words
that we come home to here

But we have agreed already
to the deaths she daily asks of us;
and in acknowledgement, did you notice?
she has marked the way with
small white feathers

Prayer for Winter

You have to be beautiful today
a voice whispers
and why today and
for whom?

Today is when the winter has not come
to bound the boundless
and spring whispers too soon
putting out yellow celandine fingers
to test if it be time
time to make love
under the tangled hedges
shining
in sudden affirmation
of surrender

Today is when soul longs for the
verge of skin
to know itself alone
alone with the past year's seed
clasped close under the cold
in the empowering dark

Today is when I long for your hands
to define me and
let me go
knowing the contours of myself
under your touch
defined by your love
held separate in it
held inside myself
waiting

Today I have to be beautiful
for you,
you, of the many dimensions
but only one name;

so that, wearing your winter coat
of stellar conjunctions and
the bitter fire of the tempering frost
and holding up to me the mirror
of the cold and January moon
you may caress my belly
with the astonishment of
snow
and I may know myself alive   alone
and you Lord of my heart
all many of you
seeded within me

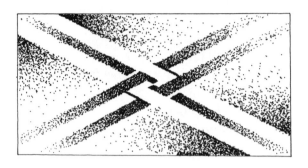

Ballad of the Woman in Green

The day was afternoon and the number seventeen
when she rose and she dressed herself all in green
behind herself invisibly she dressed in green
and she stepped in over the threshold

And the walls opened out to welcome her in
but the house was a giddy high moment of time
stretched as taut as only a heart string can
dangerously over the abyss

On the edge of herself she stood upright
testing with her toes that the rope was tight
but the one who was coming had burning feet
she saw that his feet were burning

The watchers invisibly encircling
stepped back to allow the first act to begin
and he saw clear through her eyes that she was dressed in green
and the flames flickered up to his knees

And they said: He will father himself in your love
She looked down through her body unable to move
where they held her like a bridge of stone unable to move
and the fire rose up into his heart

And he climbed inside himself 'til he stood on the crest
at the summit of himself he was a beacon ablaze
a brilliance of suffering and love all at once:
he was angel of his own annunciation

He put his foot upon the rope stretched over the drop
and it burned as he fell headlong into his life
naked and flaming, his head in a dream
and she was the darkness he fell in

Alone where she withdrew to she had curled him inside
folded the tongues of fire gently inside
her once name was Elizabeth who thought herself too old
unendowed for the busines of birthing

But now we have come to a turning point in time
where names come in to those who choose to take them on
and wherever she is now she is still dressed in green
behind herself hiddenly dressed all in green
and she gives birth to one whose name is John

Listen

Listen, listen, then you will call me here,
Listen, listen, then you will hear me sing,
Under the ground and in all the secret places.

Listen with your fingers, listen with your eyes,
Listen with your shoulders, listen with your thighs,
Listen, listen:

The leaf does not expect the dew
And the rose does not desire the sun
Nor the stranded whale crave for the tide
Nor the baking earth expect the rain . . .
They only wait, they only listen.

Listen, listen, then you will call me here,
Listen, listen, then you will hear me sing,
Along the river and in all the secret places.

Listen with your dreaming, listen with your thoughts,
Listen with your body, listen with your heart,
Listen, listen:

The warrior has no expectations
And he knows why he is waiting,
And what he gets is beyond his wildest dreams,
For there is nothing he is wanting . . .
He only waits, he only listens.

Listen, listen, then you will call me here,
Listen, listen, then you will hear me sing,
Under your heart and in all the secret places.

Listen, listen . . . . listen.

Wild Man

He took the desert by storm
and he peopled it
with the words he forbore to use
he let them slip away from him
so easily
like a woman who is used to giving birth
he let them blow away
till he was empty
as hollow as the tall dark jars
the womenfolk carry
fetching cool water
to fetch the well water home
and he wore the desert outside in
wearing its jaggedness next to his skin
that wild he was

Before Anthony or Paul
he faced them
the siren the wraith and mirage
and they used his own words
to embody themselves
and they came back to taunt and to jeer
they grappled him down
till his breath was a gasp
and they left him for dead on the hot red stones
stretched out wordlessly
under the desert stars
under the great desert moon
but he rose and took his own death on his back
gently for fear it might tumble or crack
that wild he was

And the desert turned around then
and looked at him
and she opened her secret door
his scant needs were met

abundantly
and the sun built a nest in his heart
and his words were returned to him
so resonant
the wind was amazed and took flight
in his bones they were humming
in his blood they were thrumming
guiding his feet toward home
and he walked till he came to Jordan's shore
round about and hidden was his pathway there
that wild he was

And he said I will baptize you with water
the waters of the womb he said
but one will come after
baptizing with spirit
one will come after
baptizing with spirit
one will come after
baptizing with spirit
my words are vessels
waiting for filling
vessels
but He is the wine

I do not Touch You

I have carried you inside me
for so many days and years.
I have fed you on my happiness,
I have watered you with tears;
but the path's not yet complete
which runs between your world and this:
I do not touch you with my body
but only with my voice,
I do not touch you with my body
but only with my voice.

There are flowers in my garden
of every shape and hue;
they are the loves that keep on growing
from the one seed that is you;
but time is thick between us
and I cannot see your face;
I do not touch you with my body
but only with my voice,
I do not touch you with my body
but only with my voice.

O, the heart is not a haven,
it is an ever open door,
where you died into my darkness
and left your candle there;
but the flame still keeps on growing
until it shines in every face;
I do not touch you with my body
but I can reach you with my voice,
I do not touch you with my body
but I reach you with my voice.

I will comb the skeins of memory,
I will spin them into threads
and I will weave imaginations
from this heart store full of dreams

and I will draw you from inside me
'til you are solid here beside me,
and I will touch you with my body,
touch you with my body,
yes, I will touch you with my body
and you will change me,
and you will change me,
you will change me with your words.

Blueness

There is a blueness
I'm looking at looking into
but I don't know is it sky
is it eyes;
you know how heaven
looks at you sometimes
so full and questioning and immanent
that you might drown in it upwards
if you let go?

There is a blueness between
beech bough
and bramble
speedwell, cornflower, moon blue
Giotto heaven blue, venetian
Canaletto canal blue, grecian
sea blue and blue of October
sky, washed denim blue
shades of delphinium and scilla
broadening, spreading out backwards
into somewhere undreamed of approaching
approaching this single white candle
naked and steep in the shadows
steadily burning and melting . . .
this 'I' here, awake and awaiting
the steady approach of deep ocean
dark as wine, nectar, love potion,
rising beyond those eyes, open,
and—yes it *is* eyes, I can see now—
And I am here, given already.

Take me . . .
into this blue which is darkness
lit from in front by the daylight
this blue which is seen through the sunlight
of my heart which is shining and falling

falling up into your name.
Take me deep, deeply,
oh take me . . .
take me in
into your name.

These Latter Days

When we were young
I enfolded you in blessings
when we were young
you didn't know what it meant to be alive
you were dreaming, dreaming
the stars were dreaming you down

When we were young
you were my son you were my lover
when we were young
you didn't know what it meant to be alive
that it was savage, it was beautiful
we were wild, wild together
but not free

I was your garden

But you chose to know
you chose to come here
where I die in my own waters
that are thick dark with your knowing
and I am all holes
for the sun to burn through
and I am all holes
for the sun to burn through

These latter days
you do not often come to see me
these latter days
you do not look me directly in the face
it's too uncomfortable, too uneasy
and it's close, far too close
to the bone

These latter days
you take my body and my name in vain
these days
it slips so glibly off your tongue

just an apology, just lip service
and it's chemical now, material,
no real alchemy

You took your freedom

and you chose to know
you chose to come here
where I choke in my own airspace
that is thick with your strong poisons
and I am all holes
for the sun to burn through
and I am all holes
for the sun to burn through

Is there something you forget
while you are fighting for immunity
something refined and clean
not made in your refineries
not made in your refineries:
you don't have to be immune to love
no, there's no need to be immune to love
you don't have to be immune to love
no, you are not immune to love

These latter days
you are not dreaming any more
these latter days
you're waking up to this body that you live in
and you are wondering, you are frightened
that I am close, so very close
to home

These latter days
I will not whisper any more
these latter days
you have to know what it means to be alive
that I am part of you, but it's your choice

you are free, free to choose
to take me in
you are free, free to choose
to take me in
you are free, free to choose
to take me in

I'll be your garden

Under the White Cherry

(Songs of the other woman)

This five-fold whiteness
draws me up into the heart of it,
wings arching over me
interlaced with light and blue,
and the dark boughs . . .

Everywhere I feel you
holding me up to this mystery,
mystery arching over me,
testing the readiness of each cell of me
each particle of me
ready to bud and burst
into whiteness

aching with the memory of it
aching with the work
with the re-composing of it,
of the white wedding;
when my desire died upwards
into you
into the great transcendant winged weight of you
and became
white passion . . .

and we were
what we are becoming,
a white brilliance,
from beyond the point of our
oneness, and shining back
through it to this side . . .
we were radiant white healing.

This fivefold whiteness
draws me up into the heart of it . . .

mystery of the body
becoming pure blossom,
mystery of the body . . .

rising.

Vierge Noire

Si je ne suis pas porte
je ne sais pas qui je suis;
car la porte est cadre
enfermant le vide
et le vide est le noir
que tu dois traverser,
tourné, tourbilloné par l'ouragan.

Si je ne suis pas pierre
je ne sais pas qui je suis;
car la pierre est tombe
enfermant la mort
et la mort est le seuil
que tu dois traverser,
emporté, frémissant, par les ailes
de ton desir.

Je me reconnais dans le cercle
dessiné dans le blé,
dans le dernier des cinq points noirs
dessinés sur le dé,
dans les boutons roses de l'aubépine
au printemps;
je suis le soleil à minuit,
jaillissant de l'inconscient . . .
éblouissant, nourrissant, inattendu.

Je porte ta naissance
O âme de lumiere,
lame de prière,
surgie, rayonnante, dans mes bras.

Je suis la bouche même de la terre;
et si je ne suis pas porte
à ta parole,
pierre fondamentale à ton amour,
je ne sais pas
qui je suis.

Rose in Deep Water

Hold on, we're going down
Below where words can take you.
Hold on, we're going down,
Where the pressure could break you.
Let go my hand, we shan't be parted;
Open your heart, be open hearted.
I know it's tight in here, but don't be afraid,
It's tight in here, but don't be afraid,
Yes, it's tight in here, but don't be afraid
Of the dark.

Hold on, we're going down
Below where words can take you.
Hold on, we're going down
Where the pressure could break you.
Unless you fall, I cannot touch you;
Unless you are alone, there's no way that I can reach you.
I know it hurts in here, but don't be afraid,
It hurts in here, but don't be afraid,
Yes it hurts in here, but don't be afraid
Of the pain.

This is the bridge down through yourself
To where your feet are standing;
Rose in deep water
Grows in the place where you are landing.
This is the borehole through to bedrock,
This is the borehole through to bedrock.
Rose in deep water, rose in deep water.

Hold on, we're going down
below where words can take you.
Hold on, we're going down,
where the pressure could break you.
The sun has come inside, working under cover;
If you are not first a child, how can you be my lover?
And it starts in here, where your heart is alight,

It starts in here where your heart is alight,
Yes, it starts in here, where your heart is alight,
Your heart is alight, your heart is alight
To my heart.
Rose in deep water, rose in deep water.

Resurrection

This is the Rising:
words gone,
only your light rising within me . . .
so strong.

I did not touch you then
in the garden,
my descent only beginning, my death
not yet done.

Into my deep rock darkness
split by your deed,
naked green shoot, you went before me
into my own death,
which came after;

you went before me,
trailing the sweet of spikenard
with which I annointed you,
for the redefining of the boundaries of skin,
after the blossoming of the subterranean
sprout,
womb bud, which now bursts in me
to reveal
the Rose.

Rose in deep water,
I rise with your light into myself, into my own heart
following you out of
my own death's prison.

This is the Rising:
words gone,
only your fire, Love, burning within me . . .
so strong.

And I am the garden in which we rise,
touching now right up into the body,
right up into the delicate opening verge of skin,
as one.

Easter Day
26:3:89

Gratitude

Every dawn that marries us again
draws wisdom out of a deep
inner sanctuary
you carry the keys to;
and I rise with treasures of words
unlocked to the breath,
and visions spread like silks
at some sumptuous bazaar.

The green moss of my secret ground
expands with the blessed moisture
of your true devotion, and
spreading its fronds fanwise,
patterns with burgeoning life
the sheathed dimensions
of my being.

So love empowers the unfolding
of the true gold, hiddenly,
and only love's eyes,
being blind to boundaries,
discern what shimmers into birth
beneath the opaque moment.

Initiation

You know you have gone
outside the parameters which
the metalled roads mark
and there are no markstones
for the weeping heart.

The weeping heart is held
under the leaves of time
by angels with winged eyes,
that are never closed to
your deep passage.

Your deep passage is between
the thighs of the Mother,
back into the sigilled runes of
remembrance where all is the
dark before new dawn.

The dark before new dawn
is the eye before seeing,
the larynx waiting for the
first inrush of air to usher
the first utterance.

The first utterance is a word
that comes out of the future,
spiralling inwards from the furthest
peripherous stars, informing the
world you are about to create:

and the world you are about to create
requires that you die into it
through me . . .

My voice is gentle, child,
and my touch on your brow
steadies the flame.

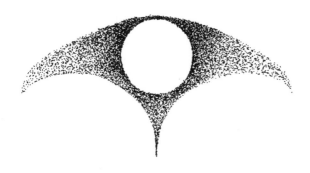

You are the pain behind my heart

You are the pain behind my heart,
the bud where the wings start growing,
the close warm pain I would not part from,
spreading release along my shoulders
like the flows of gold
spreading over your swift green hill
with the wise winds of spring,
the hill where I go to try my flight,
testing my white feathers, and
matching you wing for wing.

Curled sometimes after struggle
in the bower of my own rebirth,
I feel your fingers behind my heart,
and words drop away from this
poignant moment, where our true odyssey
begins.

108

ACKNOWLEDGEMENTS

The quotation from the Gospel of John is from *The Gospel of John*, a rendering in English by Kalmia Bittleston, published by Floris Books in 1984.

The first verse of the song *Burning River* is taken from the traditional English folk song *The Grey Cock and the Lover's Ghost*.

Magdalene and *Cup* have appeared in the magazine of the Ariadne Women's Group. *Magdalene* has also appeared in *Soluna* magazine. The song lyric *Let the Centre Hold* was in *Link-Up* magazine number 31, Summer 1987, and in TRANSFORMATION — THE POETRY OF SPIRITUAL CONSCIOUSNESS edited by Jay Ramsay and published by Rivelin Grapheme Press in 1988. *Summer* is in THE LOG BOOK, an anthology on trees, published by Roy Sadler, 51 Beech Road, Stourbridge, West Midlands. *Seek not to hold her, Soil* and *Initiation* are in IN THE GOLD OF THE FLESH — POEMS OF BIRTH AND MOTHERHOOD edited by Rosemary Palmeira and published by The Women's Press in 1990. *The Language of the Mother, She who bears the future* and *Snow* have been published in *Memes* magazine Number Three edited by Norman Jope.

Of the songs, *People of the Earth* has been recorded by myself and Rob Mehta and friends on the cassette *Green Jack 2*; and *This Time, Achilles Heel, St Jean du Puy, No Walls* and *Pathway with a Heart* are recorded on our cassette of that name—both available from Jehanne Mehta, White Lodge, 47 Bisley Old Road, Stroud, Glos. GL5 1LY.

My warm thanks to Jay Ramsay for the editing and all the encouragement, which has helped me to begin taking the poems as seriously as the songs; to Glenn Storhaug for the fine typesetting and for the help and advice on design; to my daughter Jojo for the cover photograph and the design of the lettering on the front cover; to my son Arthur for the decorations; and to all the audiences and many friends for the quality of their listening and empowerment over the years. The listener is the essential other half of all performed poems and songs, without which they do not live. Most of all I want to thank my husband Rob, whose unfailing, loving support and trust have enabled me to begin and keep on with the journey, of which these pages are only mark stones.

The Earth herself is my continual inspiration and I have no words to express my debt to her.

Other books from The Diamond Press
Putting the heart and soul back into poetry

PAPERBACKS

Carolyn Askar
Interpreting the Tree
£4.95

Valerie Denton
Dancing in the Flame
(price to be announced)

Diana Durham
Sea of Glass
£5.95

Geoffrey Godbert
Journey to the Edge of Light
£4.50
For Now
(with Jay Ramsay)
£5.95

Jay Ramsay
Psychic Poetry
£3.35
The Great Return
 Books 1-3 £7.95
 Books 4-5 £9.95

Lizzie Spring
First Things
£4.75

PAMPHLETS
(each at £2.50/£3.00)

Jenny Johnson
Towards Dawn

Jay Ramsay
The Rain, The Rain

Eric Ratcliffe
Ark

Richard Wainwright
Paeonies

Helen White
Exquisite Salmon Wish

The Diamond Press
5 Berners Mansions, 34/36 Berners Street, London WIP 3DA
Telephone 071 580 0767